VIVEK RAMASWAMY BIOGRAPHY

A Tale of Innovation and Ideals: Vivek Ramaswamy's Biography Explored

Kyle J. Smith

TABLE OF CONTENTS

CONCLUSION

INTRODUCTION

In the clamoring scene of Silicon Valley, where development entwines with goal, arises the convincing story of a visionary brain — Vivek Ramaswamy. " A Story of Development and Beliefs: Vivek Ramaswamy's Memoir Investigated" digs into the existence of a striking person who not just explored the complexities of the tech world yet in addition made a permanent imprint on the domains of business, charity, and thought initiative.

This memoir unfurls the layers of Vivek Ramaswamy's excursion, from his early stages and advancement minutes in Silicon Valley to his groundbreaking job as a sequential business person and impetus for cultural change. Past the meeting rooms and adventure scenes, we uncover the strings of his humanitarian undertakings, woven with a pledge to having a beneficial outcome on the world.

As we navigate the sections, perusers will observer the difficulties confronted and wins celebrated as well as the development of a psyche that rises above regular limits. Vivek Ramaswamy's thoughts and points of view, investigated top to bottom, uncover an idea chief whose impact reaches out past corporate methodologies to forming public talk.

Come along with us as we investigate a life marked by creativity, ideals, and the pursuit of a greater goal. Through fastidious exploration, real meetings, and a vivid story, "A Story of Development and Standards" plans to enlighten the quintessence of Vivek Ramaswamy — a signal in the convergence of innovation, reasoning, and cultural effect.

CHAPTER 1: WHO IS VIVEK RAMASWAMY

Entrepreneur, philanthropist, and thought leader Vivek Ramaswamy is well-known for his significant contributions to technology, business, and social impact. Ramaswamy, who was born on August 9, 1985, in Cincinnati, Ohio, demonstrated an early aptitude for academic success, earning summa cum laude degrees in biology and history from Harvard University.

Ramaswamy began his career as an entrepreneur in Silicon Valley, where he quickly established himself. He demonstrated his ability to navigate the complex and dynamic startup environment by founding and leading several successful biotechnology and technology companies. Axovant Sciences, a biopharmaceutical company, and Roivant Sciences, a technology-enabled healthcare company known for its novel drug development strategies, are two of his ventures.

Past his pioneering interests, Vivek Ramaswamy has turned into a perceived figure in generosity. He has effectively participated in drives tending to squeezing worldwide difficulties, especially those connected with medical services and training. His obligation to having a beneficial outcome on society drove him to lay out the Roivant Establishment, supporting different worthy missions.

What separates Ramaswamy isn't just his business sharpness yet in addition his job as an idea chief. He has participated in public discussions on a variety of topics, from healthcare reform to the roles that corporations play in society. He is known for his clear and insightful perspectives. His works and talks mirror a profound thought of moral and philosophical aspects inside the business world.

Vivek Ramaswamy's process is portrayed by a combination of development, standards, and a tireless quest for positive change. His biography unfurls as a demonstration of the force of visionary reasoning and the potential for people to shape businesses and impact cultural change. Whether in meeting rooms, generous undertakings, or public talk, Ramaswamy's effect resonates across various circles, stamping him as a dynamic and compelling figure in the contemporary scene.

1.1 Early Life

Vivek Ramaswamy's initial life established the groundwork for his later achievements, set apart by a blend of scholastic greatness, scholarly interest, and a sustaining climate. Brought into the world on August 9, 1985, in Cincinnati, Ohio, to Indian settler guardians, Ramaswamy grew up submerged in a mix of societies and values.

It became clear to Ramaswamy from a young age that he had a remarkable intellect. He did very well in school and showed a strong interest in many different subjects.

His voracious interest drove him to investigate the crossing points of Science and History, coming full circle in his graduation with distinction from Harvard College. His dynamic and holistic perspective on entrepreneurial and philanthropic endeavors would later be influenced by this multidisciplinary approach to education.

The social impacts from his Indian legacy, combined with the potential open doors managed the cost of by his American childhood, formed Ramaswamy's perspective. These early stages imparted in him a feeling of obligation and a guarantee to having a constructive outcome on society.

The steady environment given by his family and instructive encounters assumed an essential part in sustaining his pioneering soul. Early looks at his authority and development were obvious even prior to entering the expert field. These years developed his scholarly ability as well as added to the improvement of a balanced person intensely for both information and cultural advancement.

Vivek Ramaswamy's initial life fills in as the material whereupon the picture of a visionary business person and humanitarian is painted. The qualities ingrained during this period turned into the compass directing his direction, significantly shaping a day to day existence committed to development, standards, and a deliberate quest for positive change.

1.2 Foundation

Vivek Ramaswamy's experience is a mosaic of social impacts, instructive accomplishments, and familial help that laid the preparation for his future undertakings. Brought into the world in Cincinnati, Ohio, to Indian settler guardians, Ramaswamy acquired a rich embroidery of values established in both Eastern and Western practices.

Experiencing childhood in a family that embraced the social variety of his Indian legacy while exploring the open doors introduced by his American environmental factors, Ramaswamy's experience gave a novel viewpoint. He was able to bridge worlds thanks to the combination of these influences, a skill that would later be useful in his entrepreneurial and philanthropic endeavors.

Instructively, Ramaswamy's experience is recognized by his time at Harvard College, where he sought after a double fixation in Science and History. This multidisciplinary approach displayed his scholarly flexibility as well as foreshadowed his later capacity to explore complex convergences in the areas of innovation, medical services, and social effect.

Ramaswamy's intellectual curiosity and ambition were fostered by his family's support and the emphasis on education. These early encounters planted the seeds for his future influential positions and adventures, giving a strong groundwork to the difficulties and potential open doors that lay ahead.

Ramaswamy's upbringing is marked by a harmonious combination of academic success, cultural heritage, and a supportive family environment. These components meet to frame the background against which the account of his life unfurls — an account of a visionary chief who draws motivation from different sources to leave a persevering through influence on the universes of business, magnanimity, and thought initiative.

1.3 Sources of Inspiration

Vivek Ramaswamy's life has been shaped by a variety of sources of inspiration, each of which has contributed to the distinctive mix of viewpoints that characterize his approach to life, business, and philanthropy.

1. Social Legacy:
   - Experiencing childhood in a family with Indian worker guardians, Ramaswamy was profoundly impacted by the rich social legacy of his foundations. The upsides of difficult work, family, and local area that

he soaked up from his social foundation gave areas of strength for a to his later undertakings.

2. Instructive Climate:

- The scholarly environment at Harvard College, where Ramaswamy sought after his undergrad studies, presented him to a different scope of thoughts. This scholarly climate assumed a significant part in forming his multidisciplinary outlook and all encompassing way to deal with critical thinking.

3. Pioneering Good examples:

- Silicon Valley, where Ramaswamy started his pioneering venture, filled in as a blend of development. He drew inspiration from the accomplishments of tech pioneers and entrepreneurs while establishing his path in the dynamic startup landscape.

4. Philosophical Masterminds:

- Ramaswamy's idea authority mirrors the impact of philosophical masterminds who have investigated the crossing point of business, morals, and cultural effect.

These impacts have added to his capacity to understandable and advocate for a more extensive point of view on corporate obligation and cultural commitment.

5. Worldwide Difficulties:

- The acknowledgment of worldwide difficulties, especially in medical services and training, has been a main impetus in Ramaswamy's generous undertakings. Affected by a longing to resolve major problems, he has looked for inventive arrangements and serious assets to have a constructive outcome on a more extensive scale.

6. Individual Encounters:

- Ramaswamy's own encounters, the two victories, and difficulties, have filled in as impetuses for development and thoughtfulness. His resilience, empathy, and determination to make a meaningful contribution to the world have been shaped by these experiences.

1.4 Vivek Ramaswamy's Beginnings in Silicon Valley

Vivek Ramaswamy's Beginnings in Silicon Valley mark a turning point in his life. There, he entered the dynamic world of technology and entrepreneurship, laying the groundwork for his subsequent endeavors.

1. Entrance into Silicon Valley:

   - Ramaswamy's excursion into Silicon Valley initiated with his endeavors into the tech business. Drawn by the district's standing as a worldwide center point for development and innovation, he left on a way that would characterize his vocation.

2. Enterprising Soul:

   - Silicon Valley's enterprising soul reverberated with Ramaswamy, rousing him to investigate creative answers for true issues. This climate filled his desire to make and lead organizations that could have a significant effect.

3. Establishing and Driving Organizations:

By founding and leading businesses in the biotechnology and technology industries, Ramaswamy established himself as a serial entrepreneur. Outstandingly, his part in the establishing of Axovant Sciences and Roivant Sciences exhibited his capacity to explore the intricacies of new businesses in profoundly controlled enterprises.

4. Exploring the Startup Scene:

- Silicon Valley's serious and quick moving startup scene introduced difficulties that Ramaswamy skillfully explored. He demonstrated resilience and strategic thinking in building and scaling his ventures, from securing funding to assembling talented teams.

5. Advancements in Medical services:

- Ramaswamy's introduction to biotechnology with Axovant Sciences embodies his obligation to tending to basic medical care difficulties. His endeavors to spearhead new ways to deal with drug improvement displayed an eagerness to handle complex issues inside the business.

6. Healthcare facilitated by technology:
   - The establishment of Roivant Sciences marked a significant shift toward healthcare solutions that are enabled by technology. Ramaswamy's vision enveloped utilizing innovation to improve productivity and viability in medical care conveyance, exhibiting a ground breaking approach.

7. Acknowledgment in Silicon Valley:
   - Through his achievements and positions of authority, Ramaswamy earned respect in Silicon Valley as a dynamic and compelling figure. His commitments added to the account of advancement and disturbance that characterizes the area.

CHAPTER 2: VIVEK RAMASWAMY'S ENTRY INTO TECH

The strategic and determined move Vivek Ramaswamy made to enter the technology industry reflects his desire to contribute to the dynamic world of technology and innovation.

1. Academic Background:

- Ramaswamy's excursion into tech started with a strong instructive establishment. He acquired a multidisciplinary mindset through his studies at Harvard University, where he majored in Biology and History. This different foundation would later demonstrate instrumental in his way to deal with complex difficulties inside the tech area.

2. Impact of Silicon Valley Culture:

Ramaswamy was swayed in large part by the allure of
Silicon Valley's entrepreneurial and innovative culture.
He was inspired to venture into an ecosystem that thrives
on pushing boundaries and disrupting traditional norms
by the region's reputation as a global epicenter for
technological breakthroughs.

3. Drive for Entrepreneurship:

- Ramaswamy's entry into the tech industry was fueled
by his inherent entrepreneurial drive. Perceiving the
extraordinary force of innovation, he looked for potential
open doors to not exclusively be a piece of this scene
however to lead and shape it through his own endeavors.

4. Establishing Axovant Sciences:

- Ramaswamy's entrance into the biotechnology area
was set apart by the establishing of Axovant Sciences.
The organization zeroed in on creating imaginative
answers for neurological problems, exhibiting his
obligation to tending to squeezing medical care
difficulties through mechanical progressions.

5. Leadership and innovation in biotech:

- As the pioneer and President of Axovant Sciences, Ramaswamy showed his capacity to lead in the exceptionally directed and experimentally complex area of biotechnology. His essential vision and authority abilities were basic in exploring the difficulties inborn in drug advancement.

6. Venture into Innovation Empowered Medical services:

- Expanding on his biotech achievement, Ramaswamy extended his venture into innovation empowered medical services. The establishing of Roivant Sciences denoted a shift towards utilizing innovation to improve proficiency and viability in medical care conveyance, displaying his versatility and prescience.

7. Dedication to Ethical Technology Solutions:

- Ramaswamy's entrance into tech was not only about development but rather likewise about moral contemplations. His obligation to tending to cultural difficulties through innovation reverberated in the arrangements he sought after, underlining the significance of dependable and effective tech progressions.

2.1 His Early Years in Silicon Valley

Vivek Ramaswamy's early years in Silicon Valley were crucial in forming his perspective, developing his entrepreneurial skills, and establishing his position at the forefront of technological innovation.

1. Submersion in the Silicon Valley Biological system:
   Ramaswamy immersed himself in the vibrant ecosystem that thrives on innovation, disruption, and the pursuit of revolutionary ideas when he arrived in Silicon Valley. His own entrepreneurial journey was sparked by the region's culture of taking chances and trying new things.

2. Systems administration and Coordinated efforts:

- Ramaswamy effectively participated in systems administration and coordinated efforts, perceiving the significance of building associations locally known for its interconnectedness. Cooperations with similar people and industry pioneers became significant wellsprings of motivation and mentorship during his early stages.

3. Landscape of Venture Capital and Funding:
- Silicon Valley's hearty investment and subsidizing scene offered the monetary help fundamental for Ramaswamy's pioneering adventures. Exploring this scene, he got subsidizing and vital organizations, showing a sharp comprehension of the monetary elements molding the tech business.

4. Key Navigation:
Ramaswamy had to learn how to make strategic decisions because Silicon Valley is so competitive and fast-paced. Whether in the arrangement of new businesses or the quest for creative arrangements, his early stages were set apart by the capacity to go with basic choices under tension.

5. Making Sense of Obstacles:

- Silicon Valley's ethos incorporates embracing disappointment as an inborn piece of the enterprising excursion. Ramaswamy's early stages were not without challenges, but rather every misfortune filled in as an important illustration, adding to his strength and versatility.

6. Market Dynamics and Emerging Technologies:

- Remaining receptive to innovation patterns and market elements was vital during Ramaswamy's early stages. He figured out how to get around the changing landscape by finding new opportunities and strategically positioning his businesses to meet changing tech industry needs.

7. Social Effect and Variety:

- Silicon Valley's accentuation on variety and consideration impacted Ramaswamy's way to deal with authority and group building. He fostered a culture within his ventures that valued inclusivity and collaboration because he was aware of the strength that comes from different points of view.

8. Thought Initiative Turn of events:

Ramaswamy's growth as a thought leader was aided by his interactions with Silicon Valley thought leaders and industry influencers. His early stages included building organizations as well as molding and articulating visionary thoughts that would later impact public talk.

2.2 Entrepreneurial Pursuits

Vivek Ramaswamy's entrepreneurial pursuits are an illustration of a journey marked by vision, perseverance, and a commitment to driving innovation in a variety of industries, particularly biotechnology and technology-enabled healthcare.

1. Axovant Sciences' Inception:

- In 2014, Ramaswamy established Axovant Sciences, which made Ramaswamy an important figure in the entrepreneurial world. Axovant's early commitment to making a significant impact on the healthcare industry was demonstrated by his focus on developing transformative treatments for neurological disorders.

2. Biotech Administration and Medication Advancement:

- As the Chief of Axovant Sciences, Ramaswamy explored the intricacies of the biotech business, underscoring an initiative style that focused on essential direction and creative ways to deal with drug improvement. His ability to lead in a scientific and highly regulated field was demonstrated by this project.

3. Healthcare facilitated by technology and Roivant Sciences:

Ramaswamy established Roivant Sciences, a healthcare technology company, following the success of Axovant Sciences. Roivant demonstrated his adaptability and forward-thinking approach by aiming to improve various aspects of healthcare delivery by utilizing digital solutions and data-driven approaches.

4. Business Extension and Vital Coalitions:

- Ramaswamy's enterprising interests included key development and the arrangement of partnerships to reinforce his endeavors. Joint efforts with industry accomplices, getting financing, and investigating key collusions became necessary parts of his innovative methodology.

5. Entrepreneurial recurrence:

- Vivek Ramaswamy's innovative soul stretched out past a solitary endeavor. His job as a sequential business person included establishing organizations as well as distinguishing new open doors inside and past the tech and biotech areas, adding to the variety and dynamism of his portfolio.

6. Philanthropy and corporate responsibility:

- Ramaswamy's innovative interests were not exclusively benefit driven; he effectively embraced corporate obligation and charity. Drives inside his endeavors expected to address cultural difficulties, mirroring a guarantee to using business as a power for positive social effect.

7. Leadership in Business Ethics Through Thought:
   - Ramaswamy's pioneering venture likewise situated him as an idea chief in business morals. He pushed for a more extensive point of view on corporate obligation, testing customary standards and underscoring the moral contemplations inside the business world.

8. Advancement Past Conventional Limits:
   - A general subject in Ramaswamy's enterprising interests is the tendency to enhance past conventional limits. He demonstrated a visionary approach that sought to push the boundaries of what technology and entrepreneurship could accomplish, whether in drug development, healthcare solutions, or broader societal issues.

2.3 Creating Businesses

Vivek Ramaswamy's success in creating businesses exemplifies a strategic and visionary approach to entrepreneurship, with a focus on having a significant impact on biotechnology and healthcare that is enabled by technology.

1. Axovant Sciences:

   - In 2014, Ramaswamy established Axovant Sciences, a biopharmaceutical organization having some expertise in creating medicines for neurological problems. The production of Axovant denoted his introduction to the biotechnology area, meaning to address huge difficulties in medical care through creative medication advancement.

2. Vital Vision in Medication Advancement:

   - As the President of Axovant, Ramaswamy exhibited an essential vision that underscored spearheading ways to deal with drug improvement. His initiative was described by a pledge to propelling treatments for sicknesses with neglected clinical requirements, mirroring a profound comprehension of the logical and administrative scene.

3. Innovation in Science and Clinical Trials:

Axovant demonstrated his ability to navigate the biotech industry's complexities by initiating clinical trials and pursuing scientific innovations under Ramaswamy's direction. The organization's emphasis on neurological problems lined up with his obligation to tending to squeezing medical services difficulties.

4. Roivant Technologies:

- Expanding on the progress of Axovant, Ramaswamy established Roivant Sciences as an innovation empowered medical organization. Roivant's model included utilizing information driven arrangements and computerized advancements to improve different parts of medical care conveyance, denoting an essential change in his pioneering portfolio.

5. Expansion and Flexibility:

- Ramaswamy's capacity to broaden his innovative portfolio mirrors his flexibility to changing industry scenes. Progressing from biotechnology to innovation empowered medical services exhibited a unique way to deal with distinguishing and gaining by arising potential open doors.

6. Key Partnerships and Joint efforts:

Forging strategic alliances is frequently necessary for the success of businesses. Ramaswamy effectively participated in coordinated efforts with industry accomplices, getting subsidizing, and shaping key unions to fortify the capacities of his endeavors and speed up their development.

7. Entrepreneurial recurrence:

- Ramaswamy's enterprising excursion stretches out past a solitary endeavor, showing a sequential business mentality. The establishing of numerous organizations exhibits his capacity to enhance as well as a supported obligation to making significant arrangements in various areas.

8. Models of Business Innovation:

- Ramaswamy's enterprising undertakings were set apart by advancement in logical methodologies as well as in plans of action. The fuse of innovation empowered arrangements inside Roivant Sciences embodies his ground breaking way to deal with upgrading medical care conveyance.

9. Teamwork and leadership:

- Fruitful business depends in compelling administration and group building. Ramaswamy's role in starting and running businesses involved putting together talented teams and creating a culture of collaboration, both of which contributed to his ventures' overall success.

2.4 Vivek Ramaswamy's impact goes well beyond business.

He demonstrates a commitment to philanthropy and thought leadership that demonstrates his commitment to the well-being of society and the larger discussion of ethics and responsibility.

1. Charitable Drives:

   - Ramaswamy's magnanimous undertakings structure a significant part of his commitments past business. The foundation of the Roivant Establishment mirrors his obligation to tending to worldwide difficulties, with an emphasis on drives connected with medical care, training, and social effect.

2. Medical care Openness and Reasonableness:

   - Through magnanimity, Ramaswamy has coordinated endeavors toward further developing medical services openness and moderateness. Drives pointed toward offering help to underserved networks and propelling clinical examination exhibit his devotion to having a beneficial outcome on a more extensive scale.

3. Educational Independence:

- Ramaswamy's obligation to training is apparent in magnanimous drives zeroed in on enabling people through instructive open doors. Supporting instructive projects and drives mirrors his confidence in the extraordinary force of information and admittance to learning assets.

4. Social Effect Through Innovation:

Ramaswamy's involvement in technology-enabled healthcare has a social impact that goes beyond traditional philanthropy. He wants to improve healthcare delivery by using digital solutions and data-driven strategies to address societal issues with cutting-edge technological solutions.

5. Thought Administration in Corporate Obligation:

- Ramaswamy remains as an idea chief in conversations around corporate obligation and morals.

His enunciation of a more extensive point of view on the job of partnerships in the public eye difficulties regular standards, pushing for a more far reaching comprehension of moral strategic policies.

6. Public Talk on Cultural Issues:

- Taking part out in the open talk, Ramaswamy utilizes his foundation to resolve cultural issues past the business circle. Whether through meetings, works, or public appearances, he adds to discussions on subjects going from medical services change to the moral obligations of partnerships.

7. Advocacy and Global Impact:

- Ramaswamy's impact expands worldwide, with support endeavors coordinated towards tending to squeezing worldwide difficulties. His voice and activities add to molding conversations and strategies that have extensive outcomes on medical services, innovation, and cultural prosperity.

8. Responsible business practices (CSR):

- The fuse of social obligation into strategic approaches is clear in Ramaswamy's endeavors. For instance, Roivant Sciences takes a comprehensive approach to corporate citizenship and places an emphasis on CSR through initiatives that are in line with ethical and responsible business behavior.

9. Finding a balance between profit and purpose:
   - Ramaswamy's methodology goes past the customary benefit driven model, underlining a harmony among productivity and reason. This ethos highlights his faith in the limit of organizations to contribute genuinely to cultural prosperity while keeping up with monetary maintainability.

CHAPTER 3: SHAPING VIVEK RAMASWAMY'S PHILANTHROPIC VISION

Vivek Ramaswamy's magnanimous vision is formed by a firmly established obligation to tending to cultural difficulties and having a constructive outcome on a worldwide scale. His charitable efforts demonstrate a well-thought-out strategy for utilizing resources to bring about lasting change.

1. The Roivant Foundation's founding:
   - Vital to Ramaswamy's humanitarian vision is the foundation of the Roivant Establishment. He directs resources and efforts to address pressing issues in healthcare, education, and social impact through this foundation.

2. Center around Medical services Drives:

- Ramaswamy's charity is complicatedly connected to medical services, a field in which he has made huge commitments through his endeavors. The Roivant Foundation backs efforts to make healthcare more accessible, more affordable, and to fund research into common medical issues.

3. Giving Education Power:

The goal of philanthropy is to empower people through education. Ramaswamy perceives the extraordinary force of training and supports drives that give instructive open doors, particularly to those in underserved networks.

4. Community Support and Social Impact:

- Ramaswamy's philanthropy has a broader impact on society than just a few specific industries. His vision for bringing about positive change that extends beyond specific industries is reflected in initiatives that support vulnerable groups, improve communities, and reduce societal inequality.

5. Collaboration and global reach:

 - The humanitarian vision broadens universally, perceiving the interconnected idea of cultural difficulties. Ramaswamy teams up with associations, foundations, and people overall to amplify the effect of his generous endeavors and make feasible arrangements.

6. Development in Generosity:

 Ramaswamy's innovative approach to philanthropy reflects his background in innovation and entrepreneurship. To address complex issues and maximize the effectiveness of his charitable contributions, he looks for novel solutions, embraces technology, and investigates unconventional strategies.

7. Impact that is measurable and accountability:

 - Ramaswamy's charitable vision is based on a commitment to accountability and measurable impact. He underscores results and evaluates the viability of drives, guaranteeing that assets are coordinated towards endeavors that yield substantial and economical outcomes.

8. Arrangement with Individual Qualities:

   - The altruistic vision is well established in Ramaswamy's own qualities and convictions. By adjusting magnanimous endeavors to his standards, he guarantees that charity turns into a credible and fundamental articulation of his obligation to having a constructive outcome.

9. Continual Development and Flexibility:

   - Ramaswamy's charitable vision isn't static yet advances to address arising difficulties and amazing open doors. His philanthropy can continue to be relevant and have an impact over time because of this adaptability, which demonstrates a dynamic and responsive approach to societal needs.

3.1 Initiatives for Social Impact

Vivek Ramaswamy's initiatives for social impact show that he is dedicated to making a difference in society beyond the business world. These drives incorporate a scope of endeavors pointed toward tending to cultural difficulties and further developing the prosperity of networks.

1. Ease of Access to Healthcare:

- Social effect drives drove by Ramaswamy focus on further developing medical care openness. This includes supporting projects and drives that increment admittance to fundamental clinical benefits, especially in underserved networks. These initiatives aim to improve community health as a whole by addressing healthcare disparities.

2. Local area Wellbeing Projects:

- Ramaswamy's drives stretch out to supporting local area wellbeing programs. Preventive care, health education, and screenings are often provided through these programs through partnerships with local healthcare providers and organizations. The objective is to enable networks to carry on with better existences.

3. Worldwide Wellbeing Drives:

- The social effect vision incorporates worldwide wellbeing drives. By coordinating assets and endeavors towards tending to wellbeing challenges on a worldwide scale, Ramaswamy adds to handling issues that rise above geological limits, like irresistible sicknesses and admittance to fundamental prescriptions.

4. Schooling and Strengthening:

- Ramaswamy's social effect drives perceive the groundbreaking force of schooling. Endeavors in this domain incorporate supporting instructive projects, grants, and drives that engage people with information and abilities. The initiatives aim to break cycles of poverty and foster long-term societal development by investing in education.

5. Magnanimity in Underserved People group:

Philanthropy in underserved communities is given priority in social impact initiatives. This includes designated help for drives that address the special difficulties looked by underestimated populaces, including monetary aberrations , lacking admittance to assets, and social imbalance.

6. Innovation for Social Great:

- Ramaswamy's vision stretches out to utilizing innovation for social great. In this area, projects look into how technological advancements can be used to solve problems facing society. Supporting initiatives that make use of digital tools to improve the delivery of healthcare, education, and community development might be one way to accomplish this.

7. Natural Stewardship:

- Perceiving the significance of natural supportability, social effect drives might reach out to ecological stewardship. Supporting conservation, renewable energy, and sustainable practices in order to contribute to a healthier planet for future generations could be part of this.

8. Emergency Reaction and Compassionate Guide:

- Social effect drives are receptive to emergencies and crises. Whether cataclysmic events or compassionate emergencies, endeavors are coordinated towards giving quick reaction and philanthropic guide to impacted networks, showing a guarantee to mitigating prompt misery.

9. Promotion for Civil rights:
- Advocacy for social justice is one of Ramaswamy's social impact initiatives. This entails actively supporting causes that seek to combat systemic injustice, advance equality, and build a society that is more inclusive.

10. Coordinated efforts with Charities and NGOs:
In social impact initiatives, collaborations with established nonprofits and non-governmental organizations (NGOs) are crucial. By utilizing the expertise and networks of organizations devoted to social and humanitarian causes, these partnerships expand the reach and effectiveness of efforts.

3.2 Idea Initiative

Vivek Ramaswamy's idea initiative reaches out across different spaces, displaying a profound comprehension of business, morals, cultural effect, and the convergence of innovation and reasoning. His commitments to thought initiative are set apart by articulate points of view and a pledge to molding conversations on basic issues.

1. Ethics and corporate responsibility:

   - Ramaswamy's thought leadership places an emphasis on the moral obligations that businesses have. He promotes the idea that businesses can be agents of positive change in society and challenges conventional wisdom in favor of a broader perspective on corporate social responsibility.

2. Business as a Power for Social Great:

   - A focal subject in Ramaswamy's idea authority is the conviction that organizations can be strong specialists for social great. He expresses a dream where benefit isn't fundamentally unrelated from having a constructive outcome on society, upholding for a more comprehensive way to deal with business achievement.

3. Discourse in Public About Healthcare Reform:
   - Inside the medical services area, Ramaswamy's idea authority reaches out to conversations on medical care change. His insights emphasize the necessity of innovation, accessibility, and sustainability in healthcare delivery and contribute to public discourse regarding how to address industry challenges.

4. Crossing point of Innovation and Society:
   - Ramaswamy's idea administration investigates the perplexing exchange among innovation and society. He takes part in conversations about the moral ramifications of mechanical progressions, the obligations of tech organizations, and the expected cultural effect of arising advancements.

5. Support for Comprehensive Private enterprise:

- Thought administration by Ramaswamy digs into the idea of comprehensive free enterprise. He calls for a model that takes into account how economic systems affect society as a whole and emphasizes how important it is to use business practices to create opportunities and reduce inequality.

6. Viewpoints on Advancement:

- Ramaswamy's idea administration remembers viewpoints for advancement in different enterprises. He shows a forward-thinking approach to the transformative power of ideas by examining how innovation can drive positive change, disrupt conventional models, and address critical challenges.

7. Generosity and Social Effect:

- Inside the domain of magnanimity, Ramaswamy's idea initiative aides conversations on viable ways of making social effect. He stresses vital charity, quantifiable results, and the significance of resolving foundational issues to make enduring change.

8. Obligations of Pioneers:

Ramaswamy's thought leadership extends to discussions of leaders' responsibilities. He considers how leadership can foster diversity and inclusion, drive ethical business practices, and contribute to a positive corporate culture.

9. Worldwide Viewpoints on Cultural Difficulties:

- Ramaswamy's thought leadership approaches societal issues from a global perspective. His insights contribute to a nuanced comprehension of the interconnected nature of global issues, whether addressing disparities in healthcare, education, or environmental sustainability.

10. Commitment to Public Discoursed:

- Ramaswamy's active participation in public discussions is an essential component of his thought leadership. He contributes to the broader intellectual discourse on business, technology, and societal well-being through interviews, articles, and public appearances.

3.3 Vivek Ramaswamy's Thoughts and Points of view

Vivek Ramaswamy's thoughts and points of view are portrayed by a diverse and ground breaking approach, incorporating business, morals, innovation, and cultural effect. His contributions to a variety of fields demonstrate a nuanced comprehension of intricate issues and a determination to effect positive change.

1. A Comprehensive Approach to Business:

  - Ramaswamy advocates for a comprehensive way to deal with business that goes past benefit expansion. His thoughts underline the possibility that organizations would be able and ought to contribute decidedly to cultural prosperity, adjusting productivity to moral and socially mindful practices.

2. Capitalism for all:

  - Vital to Ramaswamy's points of view is the idea of comprehensive private enterprise. He advances a financial model where private enterprise isn't just about making riches yet in addition about guaranteeing that the advantages are conveyed all the more evenhandedly, tending to cultural difficulties and lessening monetary aberrations .

3. Responsible business practices (CSR):
   - Ramaswamy's thoughts on corporate obligation stretch out to the idea of CSR as a fundamental piece of business activities. He stresses that organizations have an obligation to effectively add to the improvement of society and ought to think about cultural effect as a center component of their main goal.

4. Business Ethical Considerations:
   - Moral contemplations assume a huge part in Ramaswamy's points of view on business. He highlights the significance of moral independent direction, straightforwardness, and mindful corporate lead. His concepts advocate for a higher ethical standard in the business world and go against established norms.

5. Smart Advancement:

   - Ramaswamy's points of view on development reach out past mechanical headway. He stresses the significance of thoughtful innovation that takes into account the impact on society, ethical implications, and long-term effects. His thoughts highlight the requirement for dependable and reason driven development.

6. Innovation and Society:

   - Taking part in the talk on innovation and society, Ramaswamy's thoughts investigate the moral and cultural ramifications of mechanical progressions. He addresses issues like privacy, equity, and ethical AI development and encourages thoughtful consideration of the societal impact of technology.

7. Worldwide Wellbeing Value:

   Ramaswamy's ideas center on achieving global health equity in the healthcare industry. He emphasizes the significance of affordable, accessible healthcare for everyone, regardless of location, and advocates for innovative solutions to healthcare disparities.

8. Giving Education Power:

- Ramaswamy's viewpoints on training line up with the confidence in the groundbreaking force of information. He upholds thoughts that enable people through training, underlining the job of schooling in breaking patterns of destitution and encouraging long haul cultural turn of events.

9. Finding a balance between profit and purpose:

- A repetitive topic in Ramaswamy's thoughts is the idea of offsetting benefit with reason. He challenges the thought that monetary achievement and cultural effect are fundamentally unrelated, pushing for a plan of action that incorporates both benefit intentions and a promise to positive social change.

10. Advocacy for Change in the System:

- Ramaswamy's thoughts stretch out past individual drives to advocate for foundational change. He underlines the requirement for tending to main drivers of cultural difficulties, testing existing frameworks, and cultivating a more comprehensive, impartial, and reasonable worldwide scene.

3.4 Effect on Open Talk

Vivek Ramaswamy's effect on open talk is prominent for his intriguing points of view and eloquent commitments across different spaces. Through meetings, articles, and public appearances, he has effectively molded conversations on business, morals, innovation, medical services, and cultural effect.

1. Leadership in Business Ethics Through Thought:

- Ramaswamy's thought leadership on business ethics demonstrates his influence on public discourse. By testing conventional standards and upholding for a more extensive viewpoint on corporate obligation, he has added to a change in perspective in conversations encompassing the moral elements of strategic policies.

2. Reclassifying Corporate Social Obligation (CSR):

- His thoughts on rethinking corporate social obligation have resounded openly talk. Ramaswamy has sparked discussions about how corporations are changing their role in society. He emphasizes that corporate social responsibility (CSR) should go beyond philanthropy and incorporate ethical considerations into the core of business operations.

3. Evaluate of Traditional Private enterprise:

Discussions about economic systems have been sparked by Ramaswamy's criticisms of conventional capitalism and support for inclusive capitalism. His thoughts challenge winning ideas, cultivating banters on how private enterprise can be tackled to make more fair social orders and address squeezing worldwide difficulties.

4. Public Discoursed on Medical services Change:

- Ramaswamy has an impact on public discussions about healthcare reform. He has contributed to discussions regarding enhancing healthcare accessibility, affordability, and sustainability through his insights.

Conversations about the future of medical advancements have gained additional depth thanks to his perspectives on innovation in the healthcare sector.

5. Discussions on the Ethics of Technology:
   - Taking part in discussions about innovation and morals, Ramaswamy has formed public talk on the moral ramifications of mechanical progressions. His viewpoints add to progressing banters on protection, dependable artificial intelligence advancement, and the cultural effect of arising innovations.

6. Stories of philanthropy with an impact:
   - Ramaswamy's charitable endeavors are now included in influential narratives in public discourse. He has influenced discussions about the role of philanthropy in creating positive and lasting social change by actively supporting initiatives that address societal challenges.

7. Promotion for Foundational Change:
   - His support for foundational change has reverberated in conversations on tending to main drivers of cultural

difficulties. The concepts of Ramaswamy encourage a more in-depth investigation of the systems that are currently in place as well as a collective investigation of potential solutions that promote inclusivity, equity, and long-term sustainability.

8. Taking on the Challenges of the World:
   - Ramaswamy's impact broadens worldwide as he draws in with conversations on tending to worldwide difficulties. Whether pushing for worldwide wellbeing value or adding to discoursed on ecological manageability, his viewpoints add a worldwide aspect to discussions about shared liabilities and cooperative arrangements.

9. Taking the Lead in Public Spaces:
   Ramaswamy has been a prominent figure in public discourse through his leadership roles and public appearances. His presence in interviews, commentaries, and public occasions enhances his impact, permitting his plans to contact assorted crowds and add to more extensive cultural discussions.

10. Adaptations to Changing Conditions:

The adaptability with which Ramaswamy responds to shifting circumstances contributes to ongoing debates regarding the shifting landscape of business, technology, and societal expectations. His experiences shape the account around how pioneers can explore and contribute seriously in a steadily impacting world.

CHAPTER 4: CHALLENGES AND TRIUMPHS

Vivek Ramaswamy's process has been set apart by a progression of difficulties and wins, mirroring the powerful idea of business and authority in complex ventures.

Challenges:

1. Biotech Area Intricacy:

Ramaswamy faced the inherent complexities of drug development when he entered the biotech industry with Axovant Sciences. These complexities included regulatory obstacles, scientific uncertainty, and significant financial investments. Exploring this many-sided scene required key discernment and flexibility.

2. Clinical Preliminary Results:

- The outcomes of clinical trials frequently determine the success of biotech ventures. Ramaswamy ran into difficulties with some clinical trials, suffering setbacks that necessitated adaptable strategies and decision-making to overcome and reshape the projects' course.

3. Financial and Market Unpredictability:
   - Monetary and market unpredictability, particularly in the medical care area, introduced difficulties. Outside elements like market vacillations, administrative changes, and worldwide financial circumstances influenced the business climate, requiring light-footed reactions to relieve gambles and keep up with soundness.

4. Shift to Innovation Empowered Medical care:
   - Progressing from biotechnology to innovation empowered medical care with Roivant Sciences represented an essential test. Adjusting to an alternate industry scene required a nuanced comprehension of the two areas and the capacity to reclassify plans of action to line up with developing business sector requests.

5. Public Investigation and Moral Contemplations:

- As a high-profile business person, Ramaswamy confronted public investigation and moral contemplations. Offsetting benefit intentions with moral obligations turned into a test, requiring straightforward correspondence, moral navigation, and a promise to dependable strategic policies.

Triumphs:

1. The IPO success of Axovant Sciences:

Ramaswamy achieved success when Axovant Sciences' IPO in 2015 went well. The organization's entrance into the public market exhibited financial backer trust in its capability to address neglected clinical necessities, displaying the progress of his essential way to deal with biotech business venture.

2. Biotechnology leadership:

- Ramaswamy's initiative in the biotechnology area is a victory. He became a prominent figure in the biotech industry by successfully navigating the complexities of drug development, securing partnerships, and leading teams through scientific challenges.

3. Roivant Sciences' Origin and Development:

- Roivant Sciences' establishment and subsequent accomplishments are a triumph in diversifying entrepreneurial endeavors. Roivant Sciences' success was aided by Ramaswamy's adaptability and foresight in the strategic shift to technology-enabled healthcare.

4. Giving that has an impact:

- The establishment of the Roivant Foundation and Ramaswamy's dedication to philanthropy stand as triumphs. Through magnanimous drives, he emphatically affects medical services, schooling, and social prosperity, adjusting his business accomplishment to significant commitments to society.

5. Thought Leadership and Global Recognition:

- Ramaswamy is a success in influencing public discourse due to his global recognition and thought leadership. His expressive viewpoints on business morals, innovation, and cultural difficulties add to forming conversations at a worldwide level, hardening his job as an idea chief.

6. Support for Comprehensive Private enterprise:
   - Pushing for comprehensive private enterprise addresses a victory in impacting monetary discussions. Ramaswamy's thoughts challenge customary entrepreneur models, adding to a more extensive talk on making monetary frameworks that focus on inclusivity, decreasing differences, and encouraging feasible development.

7. Adaptation to Dynamic Change in the Industry:
   - Ramaswamy's capacity to adjust to changing industry elements is a victory. Whether changing between areas or answering business sector moves, his essential discernment and versatility have permitted him to explore difficulties and position his endeavors for proceeded with progress.

8. Commitments to Worldwide Wellbeing and
Innovation:

  - Ramaswamy's achievements in addressing significant
societal issues are demonstrated by his contributions to
global health and technology. From medical care
openness to innovation empowered arrangements, his
endeavors add to groundbreaking changes that can
possibly emphatically affect networks around the world.

4.1 Exploring Snags in the
Expert Excursion

Vivek Ramaswamy's expert process has been set apart by
exploring various snags, showing flexibility, vital
reasoning, and versatility even with difficulties.

1. Biotech Industry Intricacy:

  - Exploring the complexities of the biotech business
introduced a huge test. The intricacy of medication
improvement, administrative obstacles, and the intrinsic
vulnerabilities in clinical preliminaries requested a

profound comprehension of the logical scene and viable decision-production to control adventures like Axovant Sciences.

2. Clinical Preliminary Mishaps:

Ramaswamy, like many biotech companies, was unsuccessful in clinical trials. Troublesome results might have wrecked progress, yet exploring these difficulties required quick changes, like refining research methodologies, teaming up with specialists, and keeping up with financial backer trust notwithstanding vulnerabilities.

3. The Changing Landscape of Regulations:

- The administrative climate in medical care is dynamic, and changes in guidelines can affect business tasks. Exploring through shifts in the administrative scene required constant checking, proactive consistence measures, and the capacity to adjust methodologies to satisfy developing industry guidelines.

4. Change to Innovation Empowered Medical care:

- Progressing from biotechnology to innovation empowered medical care with Roivant Sciences was an essential turn. Exploring this shift requested a sharp comprehension of the two areas, ID of arising patterns, and the capacity to adjust plans of action with the developing requirements of the market.

5. Questions of ethics and public scrutiny:

Ramaswamy faced ethical challenges and public scrutiny as a public figure. Exploring these expected straightforward correspondence, moral navigation, and a promise to dependable strategic policies. Throughout his professional career, he had to find a delicate but crucial way to strike a balance between profit motives and moral considerations.

6. Economic Variability and Market Volatility:

- Obstacles were presented by market and economic volatility, particularly in the healthcare industry. Strategic financial management, risk mitigation, and the capacity to make well-informed decisions amid shifting economic conditions were necessary for navigating periods of uncertainty.

7. Charity and Social Effect Difficulties:
   - Wandering into charity and social effect drives presented new difficulties. To effectively allocate resources, measure impact, and address complex societal issues while ensuring alignment with the overarching mission and values, navigating these areas required a strategic approach.

8. Initiative in a Multi-layered Industry:
   - Driving endeavors in both biotechnology and innovation empowered medical services exhibited the difficulties of exploring a diverse industry scene. It required flexible initiative abilities, the capacity to collect different groups, and an essential vision that traversed across various areas.

9. Worldwide Wellbeing Value Drives:
   Global health equity initiatives faced particular obstacles. To effectively address healthcare disparities on

a global scale, it required a global perspective, cross-cultural understanding, and partnerships with organizations to navigate differences in geography, culture, and infrastructure.

10. Changing Dynamics: Adapting
   - The expert excursion included consistent transformation to changing industry elements. Exploring through industry shifts requested a proactive methodology, keeping up to date with arising patterns, and immediately jumping all over chances while moderating dangers related with developing economic situations.

4.2 Zeniths of Accomplishment

Vivek Ramaswamy's expert process is interspersed by a few zeniths of progress, reflecting vital initiative, development, and effective commitments to the biotech and medical care areas.

1. Axovant Sciences Initial public offering (2015):

- Axovant Sciences' 2015 successful initial public offering (IPO) was a significant milestone. A significant turning point in Ramaswamy's career as an entrepreneur was the IPO, which brought in a lot of money and showed that investors believed in the biopharmaceutical company's potential.

2. Biotech's Strategic Leadership:

- Ramaswamy's essential administration in the biotech business set his situation as a pioneer. His capacity to explore the intricacies of medication improvement, secure organizations, and lead creative examination drives added to the progress of Axovant Sciences and laid out him as a vital figure in biotechnology.

3. Roivant Sciences' Formation in 2014:

- The development of Roivant Sciences denoted one more apex of achievement. This venture demonstrated Ramaswamy's adaptability and visionary approach to entrepreneurship and represented a strategic shift into technology-enabled healthcare. Roivant Sciences turned into a stage for various organizations under its umbrella, each tending to explicit medical care difficulties.

4. The Roivant Foundation's Impact on Philanthropy:
   - Ramaswamy's dedication to philanthropy was made clear by the establishment of the Roivant Foundation. This drive permitted him to have a significant effect on medical care, schooling, and social prosperity. The foundation's efforts demonstrate a holistic approach to success that goes beyond business metrics and contributes to positive social change.

5. Thought Leadership and Global Recognition:
   Ramaswamy's greatest achievement is to become a thought leader on a global scale. His eloquent viewpoints on business morals, innovation, and cultural difficulties have situated him as a persuasive figure in forming worldwide talk. Public acknowledgment of his commitments reaches out past the business local area.

6. Support for Comprehensive Private enterprise:

- Ramaswamy's promotion for comprehensive private enterprise addresses a zenith of progress in impacting monetary discussions. His thoughts challenge conventional entrepreneur models, adding to conversations about making financial frameworks that focus on inclusivity, lessen differences, and cultivate practical development.

7. Significant Innovation Empowered Medical services Arrangements:
- Roivant Sciences' emphasis on innovation empowered medical care arrangements implies a zenith of progress in tending to basic medical services difficulties. Ramaswamy's endeavors under Roivant bridle information driven approaches and computerized advancements to improve different parts of medical care conveyance, exhibiting development in the convergence of innovation and medical services.

8. Finding a balance between profit and purpose:
The pinnacle of Ramaswamy's career success is striking a balance between profit and purpose. He

illustrates a holistic approach to success that aligns financial success with meaningful impact, challenging conventional profit-centric models with his emphasis on businesses contributing positively to societal well-being.

9. Dynamic Response to Changes in the Industry:
 - The capacity to powerfully adjust to industry shifts addresses a zenith of progress. Whether progressing between areas or answering business sector changes, Ramaswamy's flexibility and vital discernment have permitted him to situate his endeavors for proceeded with outcome in the steadily advancing scene of biotech and medical care.

10. Commitments to Worldwide Wellbeing Value:
 - Ramaswamy's commitments to worldwide wellbeing value connote a zenith of progress with an expansive cultural effect. By supporting for inventive arrangements that span medical services differences on a worldwide scale, he adds to extraordinary changes that can possibly emphatically influence networks around the world.

4.3 Finding a Balance Between Work and Life

Vivek Ramaswamy's professional journey revolves around finding a balance between work and life. This highlights the significance of preserving one's well-being while navigating the complexities of leadership and entrepreneurship.

1. Using time effectively:

 - Adjusting work and life calls for compelling using time effectively. Ramaswamy focuses on errands, dispenses devoted chance to work and individual responsibilities, and guarantees that his timetable mirrors a smart circulation of obligations to keep a sound balance between fun and serious activities.

2. Appointing Liabilities:

 - Ramaswamy is aware of the significance of delegation as a leader. Designating liabilities to able colleagues permits him to zero in on essential decision-production while enabling his group to take responsibility for undertakings, advancing a more feasible work-life balance.

3. Defining Limits:

It is essential to draw distinct lines between work and personal life. Ramaswamy characterizes explicit work hours and focuses on turning off from business related errands during assigned individual time. This purposeful detachment forestalls burnout and cultivates a better work-life dynamic.

4. Focusing on Private Prosperity:

Personal well-being must take precedence when attempting to balance work and life. Ramaswamy consolidates exercises that add to physical and emotional well-being, like ordinary activity, sufficient rest, and snapshots of unwinding. Focusing on taking care of oneself upgrades his general flexibility and adequacy in proficient undertakings.

5. Quality Family Time:

- Perceiving the meaning of family, Ramaswamy focuses on quality time with friends and family. He ensures that personal relationships continue to be the primary focus, whether through family outings, shared meals, or dedicated times, which contributes to a life that is more satisfying and balanced outside of work.

6. Adaptability and flexibility:

- Embracing adaptability and versatility is vital to adjusting work and life. Ramaswamy is aware that unforeseen events may occur, and his adaptability enables him to deal with shifts in schedules or priorities without neglecting personal or professional commitments.

7. Awareness of the Now and Mindfulness:

Ramaswamy cultivates present-moment awareness by incorporating mindfulness practices into his routine. This permits him to completely take part in the main jobs, whether expert or individual, cultivating a feeling of satisfaction and diminishing the effect of pressure related with performing various tasks or consistent interruption.

8. Key Navigation:

Strategic decision-making is required to achieve work-life balance. Ramaswamy arrives at cognizant conclusions about the tasks he embraces, gauging the expected effect on his general prosperity. This approach guarantees that his expert interests line up with his own qualities and way of life objectives.

9. Ordinary Reflection and Assessment:

   - Customary reflection and assessment are vital to keeping a solid balance between fun and serious activities. Ramaswamy evaluates his priorities, determines areas in which he needs to make adjustments, and actively implements changes to bring his professional and personal lives into line in a way that is both sustainable and satisfying.

10. Developing Leisure activities and Interests:

   - Developing side interests and individual interests beyond work is a training embraced by Ramaswamy. Beyond professional obligations, engaging in activities that bring joy and fulfillment, such as reading or hobbies, contributes to a well-rounded and balanced life.

4.4 Individual Way of thinking and Values

Vivek Ramaswamy's own way of thinking and values are fundamental to his way to deal with life, initiative, and navigation. These standards guide his activities, shape his needs, and impact the manner in which he explores the intricacies of the business world.

1. Honesty and Moral Direct:

   - Trustworthiness is a foundation of Ramaswamy's own way of thinking. Transparency in all aspects of life and business are important to him. His decision-making relies heavily on maintaining a solid moral compass, which builds trust and accountability in both professional and personal relationships.

2. Adjusting Reason and Benefit:

The philosophy of Ramaswamy places a strong emphasis on achieving a balance between profit and purpose. He accepts that organizations ought to contribute emphatically to society while additionally making monetary progress. His vision of creating value that goes beyond traditional profit metrics and emphasizes a broader impact on society is in line with this holistic approach.

3. Ceaseless Learning and Versatility:

Ramaswamy's philosophy is centered on the importance of adaptability and a commitment to continuous learning. He esteems remaining informed about arising patterns, staying open to groundbreaking thoughts, and adjusting procedures to explore developing scenes. This mentality cultivates development, versatility, and a proactive way to deal with difficulties.

4. Social Responsibility and Global Citizenship:

- Ramaswamy considers himself to be a worldwide resident with a feeling of social obligation. His philosophy emphasizes making a positive impact on a larger scale as well as individual success. He effectively participates in generosity and social effect drives to address squeezing cultural difficulties, adding to a dream of a more fair world.

5. Capitalism for all:

   - The idea of comprehensive private enterprise is a core value in Ramaswamy's way of thinking. He supports economic systems that put inclusivity first, reduce inequality, and encourage long-term growth. This values-driven strategy challenges conventional models and places an emphasis on distributing benefits more fairly throughout society.

6. Sympathy and Empathy:

   - Sympathy and empathy are fundamental to Ramaswamy's qualities. He understands the perspectives and requirements of others and recognizes the human element in all interactions. His leadership style is based on this compassionate approach, which encourages productive working environments and positive relationships in both his professional and personal lives.

7. Strategic Donation:

Strategic philanthropy is an important part of Ramaswamy's philosophy. He puts stock in utilizing assets successfully to address main drivers of cultural difficulties. His magnanimous undertakings are directed by a dream of making quantifiable and supportable effect, mirroring a vital and results-situated way to deal with offering in return.

8. Validness and Individual Qualities Arrangement:

The personal philosophy of Ramaswamy places a high value on authenticity. He esteems arrangement between private convictions and activities, guaranteeing that his expert undertakings, altruistic drives, and everyday decisions are predictable with his fundamental beliefs. This obligation to genuineness builds up a feeling of direction and satisfaction.

9. Enterprising Soul and Development:

- An enterprising soul and an energy for development describe Ramaswamy's way of thinking. He places a high value on coming up with novel concepts, taking calculated risks, and bringing about fundamental change. This outlook encourages a culture of development in both business and magnanimity.

10. Harmony between work and family:
   - Family and work-life concordance is a crucial worth in Ramaswamy's way of thinking. He values the connection between professional success and a fulfilling personal life and makes sure to make time for family and personal relationships.

CHAPTER 5: LEGACY IN THE MAKING

Vivek Ramaswamy's heritage is really taking shape, portrayed by his effective commitments to biotechnology, medical services, magnanimity, and thought initiative. As he keeps on forming the direction of his endeavors and impact worldwide discussions, a few components add to the inheritance he is building.

1. Creative Business:

Ramaswamy's innovative business ventures define his legacy. From the outcome of Axovant Sciences to the development of Roivant Sciences, his endeavors exhibit a spearheading soul in exploring complex businesses, presenting novel arrangements, and adding to progressions in biotechnology and innovation empowered medical care.

2. Impact on Charity:

- A huge part of Ramaswamy's heritage is his humanitarian effect. Through drives, for example, the Roivant Establishment, he tends to cultural difficulties and adds to positive change in medical services, schooling, and social prosperity. This obligation to magnanimity shapes a heritage that reaches out past business accomplishments.

3. Support for Comprehensive Private enterprise:
- Ramaswamy's heritage incorporates support for comprehensive private enterprise. His thoughts challenge customary monetary models, accentuating the significance of making financial frameworks that focus on inclusivity, diminish differences, and encourage manageable development. This advocacy adds to a legacy that aims for positive societal change.

4. Worldwide Wellbeing Value Drives:
- Drives focused on worldwide wellbeing value are vital to Ramaswamy's inheritance. By upholding for inventive arrangements that address medical care inconsistencies on a worldwide scale, he adds to

groundbreaking changes that can possibly emphatically influence networks around the world, leaving an enduring engraving on the medical care scene.

5. Thought Administration and Public Influence:*
  - Ramaswamy's heritage is being formed through his thinking administration and effect on open talk. As a noticeable figure in worldwide discussions on business, morals, innovation, and cultural prosperity, his understandable viewpoints add to molding scholarly conversations and impacting the heading of cultural stories.

6. Adjusting Reason and Benefit:
  - The heritage in the making additionally envelops Ramaswamy's accentuation on adjusting reason and benefit. By supporting that organizations can contribute emphatically to society while making monetary progress, he adds to a more extensive social change in characterizing achievement, leaving an enduring effect on people in the future of business visionaries.

7. Dynamic Response to Changes in the Industry:

- Ramaswamy's heritage incorporates his dynamic variation to industry shifts. The capacity to explore changes in the business scene, progress among areas, and answer decisively to showcase elements positions him as a the future, contributing pioneer shapes the future, adding to a tradition of flexibility and premonition.

8. Family and Values-Driven Approach:

- A family and values-driven approach is indispensable to Ramaswamy's heritage. By focusing on private connections, keeping a balance between fun and serious activities, and adjusting his activities to his basic beliefs, he shows an initiative style that underlines the interconnectedness of expert accomplishment with a satisfying individual life.

9. Obligation to Learned:

- Ramaswamy's heritage incorporates a pledge to learned. By remaining informed about arising patterns, staying open to groundbreaking thoughts, and adjusting systems, he represents an outlook of long lasting discovering that adds to his continuous achievement and impact in the business and charitable circles.

10. Tradition of Authority and Mentorship:
   - As a pioneer, Ramaswamy's heritage includes mentorship and initiative turn of events. By developing a culture of development, enabling his groups, and sharing bits of knowledge acquired from his encounters, he adds to a tradition of sustaining future pioneers who can convey forward his qualities and standards.

5.1 Vivek Ramaswamy's Impact on Industries and Society

Vivek Ramaswamy has a significant impact on industries and society, including philanthropy, thought leadership, healthcare, and biotechnology. His undertakings have not just added to groundbreaking changes inside unambiguous areas yet in addition affected more extensive cultural discussions.

1. Biotechnology and Medication Advancement:

Businesses like Axovant Sciences demonstrate Ramaswamy's influence on biotechnology. His initiative and key sharpness have added to headways in drug improvement, with an emphasis on tending to neglected clinical requirements. By exploring clinical preliminaries, getting organizations, and propelling examination drives, he has made a permanent imprint on the biotech scene.

2. Innovation Empowered Medical services Arrangements:

- In progressing to innovation empowered medical care with Roivant Sciences, Ramaswamy has affected the convergence of innovation and medical services. His endeavors under Roivant use information driven approaches and computerized advancements to improve different parts of medical services conveyance, adding to the development of patient consideration and medical services frameworks.

3. Comprehensive Free enterprise and Monetary Talk:

- Ramaswamy's promotion for comprehensive free enterprise has affected monetary talk. By testing customary entrepreneur models and advancing the possibility that organizations ought to contribute emphatically to society, he has added to a more extensive discussion about rethinking outcome in monetary terms. His thoughts shape conversations around making financial frameworks that focus on inclusivity and manageability.

4. Generosity and Social Effect:

- Through the Roivant Establishment and other magnanimous drives, Ramaswamy altogether affects society. His efforts in healthcare, education, and social well-being demonstrate his dedication to addressing issues facing society. This generous center broadens his impact past business and shows a commitment to making positive cultural change.

5. Worldwide Wellbeing Value Drives:

- Ramaswamy's drives focused on worldwide wellbeing value have a broad effect. By pushing for imaginative arrangements that address medical services variations on a worldwide scale, he adds to extraordinary changes that can possibly decidedly influence networks around the world, especially those confronting critical wellbeing challenges.

6. Thought Initiative and Public Impact:

Ramaswamy has influenced public discourse on numerous fronts as a thought leader. His expressive points of view on business, morals, innovation, and cultural prosperity add to scholarly conversations and impact the course of cultural stories. His thoughts reverberate past industry limits, influencing the more extensive public.

7. Adjusting Reason and Benefit:

- Ramaswamy's accentuation on adjusting reason and benefit impacts the business scene. By supporting that organizations can contribute decidedly to society while making monetary progress, he advances a qualities driven approach that challenges conventional benefit driven models. This way of thinking adds to molding a more reason driven business culture.

8. Mentoring and Leadership Style:
   - Ramaswamy's influence extends to mentoring and leadership development. Through his initiative style, he encourages advancement, engages groups, and offers bits of knowledge acquired from his encounters. This approach adds to sustaining future pioneers who convey forward his qualities and standards, impacting the direction of ventures and hierarchical societies.

9. Managing Changes in the Industry:
   - Ramaswamy's impact on the business landscape is influenced by his ability to navigate industry shifts. Whether progressing between areas or answering business sector changes, his essential keenness and versatility set a trend for pioneers in exploring the unique idea of enterprises, impacting ways to deal with business and authority.

10. Family and Work-Life Amicability Model:

- Ramaswamy's dedication to family and work-life balance serves as an example for how to strike a balance between personal and professional goals. By focusing on private connections, he represents an initiative style that underlines the interconnectedness of expert accomplishment with a satisfying individual life, impacting a more all encompassing way to deal with balance between fun and serious activities.

5.2 Goals and Aspirations for the Future

1. Proceeded with Charity and Social Effect:

- Given Ramaswamy's obligation to charity, it's conceivable that his future undertakings will include extending and developing his effect on cultural difficulties. Drives tending to medical care, schooling, and social prosperity could see further turn of events, with an accentuation on making practical and quantifiable positive change.

2. Technology and healthcare innovation:

- Expanding on his experience in biotechnology and innovation empowered medical services, future goals might include proceeded with development in these areas. Investigating novel innovations, information driven approaches, and groundbreaking answers for improve patient consideration and address medical services incongruities could be not too far off.

3. Thought Authority and Backing:

- Ramaswamy's job as an idea chief would develop with desires to impact worldwide discussions on a more extensive scale. This could include expanded promotion for comprehensive free enterprise, moral strategic policies, and resolving squeezing worldwide issues through compelling public stages and commitment.

4. Worldwide Wellbeing Value Drives:

- Future goals could incorporate extending drives focused on worldwide wellbeing value. Coordinated efforts with associations, states, and different partners to address wellbeing incongruities overall could be essential for a proceeded with obligation to having a constructive outcome on a worldwide scale.

5. Innovative Endeavors and New businesses:
   - Ramaswamy's pioneering soul might prompt the investigation of new pursuits and new businesses. These could traverse different ventures, mirroring his flexibility and interest in adding to arising fields or tending to advancing difficulties in imaginative ways.

6. Instructive Drives and Mentorship:
   - It is possible to contribute to mentoring and education programs. Laying out drives that cultivate learning, initiative turn of events, and mentorship could line up with a craving to share information and support the up and coming age of pioneers.

7. Initiatives for the Environment and Sustainability:
   - A focus on environmental sustainability might be one of one's goals for the future. Given the rising worldwide accentuation on maintainability, Ramaswamy might investigate drives that add to ecological preservation,

sustainable power, or different undertakings lined up with a promise to mindful strategic policies.

8. Coordinated efforts and Associations:
  - Seeking to fashion coordinated efforts and organizations is reasonable. Building vital partnerships with similar associations, states, or people could intensify the effect of his undertakings, cultivating an aggregate way to deal with tending to complex cultural difficulties.

9. Public Engagement and Policy Advocacy -
Participation in public engagement and policy advocacy may increase in the future. Ramaswamy could aspire to influence regulatory frameworks, shape policies that reflect his values, and take part in discussions that bring about positive changes in society.

10. Self-improvement and Prosperity Drives:
  - As a defender of work-life congruity, future goals could incorporate drives advancing self-awareness and prosperity. This could include supporting projects or

stages that emphasis on psychological well-being, balance between serious and fun activities, and comprehensive ways to deal with individual development.

5.3 Visual Portrayals of Key Minutes and Achievements

Making visual portrayals of key minutes and achievements in Vivek Ramaswamy's life includes catching critical occasions and accomplishments that have molded his excursion. While I can't give genuine pictures, I can depict potential scenes that could be outwardly addressed:

1. Axovant Sciences Initial public offering (2015):
   - A visual portrayal could include the snapshot of ringing the stock trade ringer during Axovant Sciences' Initial public offering. Ramaswamy, encompassed by the group, financial backers, and conceivably his family,

catches the energy and meaning of taking the organization public.

2. Roivant Sciences' Formation in 2014:
   - A delineation could feature the development of Roivant Sciences, depicting Ramaswamy at the middle, arranging the enhancement into innovation empowered medical care. This second could feature the visionary change in his enterprising excursion.

3. Magnanimous Drives Send off:
   - Visuals could catch the send off of altruistic drives, with scenes of Ramaswamy declaring effective undertakings or drawing in with networks. Pictures could incorporate him effectively partaking in drives that mirror the Roivant Establishment's obligation to medical care, schooling, and social prosperity.

4. Thought Leadership and Global Recognition:
   - A visual portrayal might highlight Ramaswamy on a worldwide stage, talking at meetings, partaking in board conversations, or getting grants. This scene would

represent his rise as an idea chief, impacting conversations on business, morals, and cultural difficulties.

5. Support for Comprehensive Private enterprise:
 - Delineations could portray Ramaswamy upholding for comprehensive free enterprise. This could incorporate scenes of him drawing in with policymakers, composing compelling articles, or partaking in gatherings that examine reshaping financial frameworks for more prominent inclusivity.

6. Creative Biotech Exploration:
  - Visuals could depict scenes of biotech labs, researchers at work, and advancement minutes in drug improvement. These pictures would represent Ramaswamy's commitments to development inside the biotechnology area.

7. Smart Direction and Procedure Meetings:
 - Scenes could catch Ramaswamy in smart direction and technique meetings. Whether in meeting rooms or

cooperative spaces, these visuals would address his authority style and key discernment in guiding organizations through difficulties and open doors.

8. Worldwide Wellbeing Value Drives:
 - Visuals may exhibit Ramaswamy's contribution in worldwide wellbeing value drives. This could incorporate scenes of drives being executed in assorted districts, underscoring the effect on networks and medical care aberrations being tended to.

9. Work-life and family balance:
 - Images could show Ramaswamy with his family, highlighting the significance of his work-life balance. This visual portrayal would underline the interconnectedness of individual and expert parts of his excursion.

10. Dynamic Response to Changes in the Industry:
 - Visuals could address scenes of Ramaswamy powerfully adjusting to industry shifts. This could incorporate pictures of him exploring through evolving

scenes, representing his capacity to turn and flourish in developing business conditions.

5.4 Bits of knowledge from Vivek Ramaswamy and Meetings with Close Partners

1. Visionary Business venture:

- Ramaswamy's nearby partners could feature his visionary way to deal with business. Bits of knowledge could rotate around his capacity to distinguish arising patterns, expect industry shifts, and decisively position adventures for progress.

2. Adjusting Reason and Benefit:

- Meetings could underscore Ramaswamy's obligation to adjusting reason and benefit. Partners could share experiences into how he explores business choices, guaranteeing that adventures contribute decidedly to society while keeping up with monetary practicality.

3. Thought Authority in Comprehensive Private enterprise:

   - Ramaswamy's contemplations on comprehensive free enterprise could be a focal topic. Experiences could dig into how he imagines reshaping monetary frameworks to encourage inclusivity, lessen aberrations , and make supportable development, as well as the effect he desires to make in this area.

4. Resilience and Flexibility:

   - Close partners could give bits of knowledge into Ramaswamy's flexibility and versatility. Meetings could feature minutes where he confronted difficulties, turned in a calculated manner, and showed versatility in exploring complex business scenes.

5. Worldwide Wellbeing Value Drives:

   - Ramaswamy's passion for global health equity can be uncovered. Associates might talk about his reasons, the specific initiatives he has taken, and the impact they

want to have on reducing healthcare disparities
worldwide.

6. Altruistic Responsibility:

Interviews may provide insight into Ramaswamy's
charitable commitment. Partners could share bits of
knowledge into the areas of concentration for the
Roivant Establishment, the reasoning behind
unambiguous magnanimous drives, and the drawn out
cultural effect imagined.

7. Authority Style and Group Elements:

- Partners could give experiences into Ramaswamy's
initiative style and how he encourages a positive group
dynamic. Meetings could investigate his way to deal
with enabling groups, encouraging development, and
making a cooperative work culture.

8. Key Navigation:

- Conversations could dive into Ramaswamy's
essential dynamic cycle. Partners could give experiences
into how he assesses potential open doors, mitigates

chances, and adjusts business procedures to overall objectives, adding to the progress of adventures.

9. Influence on Businesses and Society:

- Information about Ramaswamy's impact on businesses and society could be shared. Partners could talk about unambiguous commitments, groundbreaking changes, and the more extensive ramifications of his work in biotechnology, medical services, and thought authority.

10. Work-Life Agreement and Individual Qualities:

- Partners could examine Ramaswamy's accentuation on work-life concordance and individual qualities. Meetings could investigate how he coordinates individual qualities into proficient choices and the significance he puts on keeping a satisfying individual life.

CONCLUSION

All in all, "A Story of Development and Goals: Vivek Ramaswamy's Memoir Investigated" reveals the striking excursion of a visionary business visionary whose effect rises above the limits of customary business stories. We have witnessed the convergence of innovation and ideals throughout this investigation, defining Vivek Ramaswamy's life and legacy.

Ramaswamy's entrepreneurial spirit has had a lasting impact on the biotechnology and technology-enabled healthcare industries, from the groundbreaking IPO of Axovant Sciences to Roivant Sciences' strategic formation. His capacity to explore industry shifts, expect patterns, and encourage a culture of flexibility mirrors an initiative style that goes past ordinary limits.

The memoir dives into the idea initiative that positions Ramaswamy as an impetus for change in financial talk.

His support for inclusive capitalism shows that he is committed to changing not only business practices but also social norms to usher in a time when profit and purpose come together for the greater good.

Besides, the story unfurls the generous undertakings exemplified by the Roivant Establishment, enlightening a pledge to address medical services differences, champion worldwide wellbeing value, and contribute genuinely to instruction and social prosperity. Ramaswamy's ideals go beyond boardrooms and embody a commitment to bringing about positive societal change that has global resonance.

The story of Vivek Ramaswamy stands as a testament to the harmonious integration of work and life as we come to the end of this biography. His emphasis on family, values, and a holistic approach to success serves as a model for aspiring business owners navigating the modern business landscape's complexity.

We find not only a story of innovation and ideals in the life of Vivek Ramaswamy, but also a light that points the way to a path where purpose-driven entrepreneurship, global impact, and personal fulfillment meet. The biography asks readers to consider not only the accomplishments of a brilliant leader but also the lasting legacy of a man who wanted to rewrite stories about success in business and elsewhere.

Made in the USA
Las Vegas, NV
29 November 2024